KNOCK-KNOCK JOKES

For Kids of All Ages

SWEETWATER
PRESS

Knock-Knock Jokes

Copyright © 2006 Sweetwater Press

Produced by Cliff Road Books

All rights reserved. With the exception of brief quotations in critical reviews or articles, no part of this work may be reproduced or transmitted in any form or by any means, electronic or mechanical, including photocopying, recording, or any information storage and retrieval system, without permission in writing from the publisher.

ISBN-13: 978-1-58173-600-7
ISBN 1-58173-600-2

Book design by Pat Covert
Illustrations by Tim Rocks

Printed in the U.S.

KNOCK-KNOCK JOKES

For Kids of All Ages

SWEETWATER PRESS

Knock, knock.
Who's there?
Athena!
Athena who?

Athena reindeer landing on your roof!

Knock, knock.
Who's there?
Asa!
Asa who?
Asa rule, I don't tell!

Knock, knock.
Who's there?
Arthur!
Arthur who?
Arthur any more cookies
in the canister?

Knock, knock.
Who's there?
Annie!
Annie who?
Annie one you like.

Knock, knock.
Who's there?
Control freak.
Now-you say, "Control freak WHO?"

Knock, knock.
Who's there?
Izzy!
Izzy who?
Izzy mom in?

Knock, knock.
Who's there?
Latin!
Latin who?
Latin me in would be a nice idea!

Knock, knock.
Who's there?
Adolf.
Adolf who?

Adolf ball hit me in da mouth and dats why I talk this way!

Knock, knock.
Who's there?
Lettuce.
Lettuce who?
Lettuce in already. Why do you think we're knocking?

Knock, knock.
Who's there?
Little old lady.
Little old lady who?
I like your yodeling.

Knock, knock.
Who's there?
Owl goes.
Owl goes who?
That's right!

Knock, knock.
Who's there?
Spell.
Spell who?
W-H-O.

Knock, knock.

Who's there?

Yah.

Yah who?

If you're that excited
about a person
at the door,
imagine a phone call!

KNOCK, KNOCK.
WHO'S THERE?
ARNOLD!
ARNOLD WHO?

ARNOLD FRIEND YOU HAVEN'T SEEN FOR YEARS!

KNOCK, KNOCK.
WHO'S THERE?
WATER.
WATER WHO?
WATER YOU DOING?

KNOCK, KNOCK.
WHO'S THERE?
HOWARD.
HOWARD WHO?
HOWARD I KNOW?

Knock, knock.
Who's there?
Snow.
Snow who?
Snow use, I forgot my name again!

Knock, knock.
Who's there?
Isadore.
Isadore who?
Isadore made out of wood?

Knock, knock.
Who's there?
Scott.
Scott who?
Scott nothing to do with you!

Knock, knock.
Who's there?
Zizi!
Zizi who?
Zizi when you know how!

Knock, knock.
Who's there?
Amos!
Amos who?

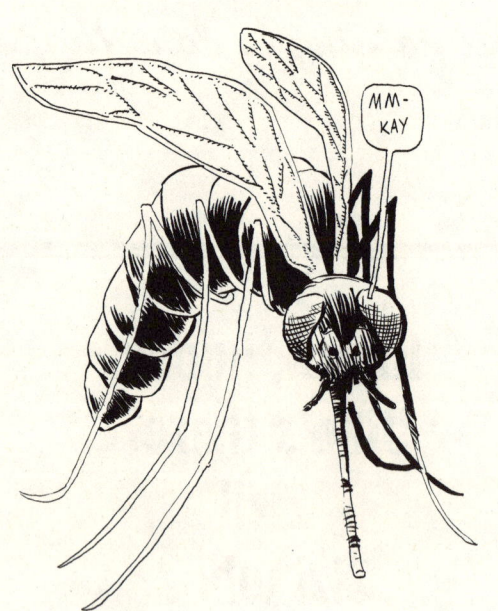

Amos quito!

KNOCK, KNOCK.
WHO'S THERE?
ALEC!
ALEC WHO?
ALEC-TRICITY. ISN'T THAT A SHOCK!

KNOCK, KNOCK.
WHO'S THERE?
ALEX!
ALEX WHO?
ALEX THE QUESTIONS ROUND HERE!

Knock, knock.
Who's there?
Albee!
Albee who?
Albee a monkey's uncle!

Knock, knock.
Who's there?
Al!
Al who?
Al give you a kiss if you open this door!

Knock, knock.
Who's there?
Boo.
Boo who?

Don't cry, it's just a joke!

Knock, knock.
Who's there?
Goat.
Goat who?
Goat to the door and find out!

Knock, knock.
Who's there?
Phyllis.
Phyllis who?
Phyllis up a cup of water!

KNOCK, KNOCK.
WHO'S THERE?
CAMILLA.
CAMILLA WHO?
CAMILLA MINUTE.

KNOCK, KNOCK.
WHO'S THERE?
ABBE.
ABBE WHO?
ABBE STUNG ME ON THE NOSE!

Knock, knock.
Who's there?
Repeat.
Repeat who?
Who Who Who!

Knock, knock.
Who's there?
Ali.
Ali, who?
Ali-ttle old man who can't reach the doorbell!

Knock, knock.
Who's there?
Gorilla.
Gorilla who?
Gorilla me a hamburger,
I'm hungry.

Knock, knock.
Who's there?
Cash!
Cash who?
I knew you were nuts!

Knock, knock.
Who's there?
Cow.
Cow who?

Cow that interrupts people!

Knock, knock.
Who's there?
Adelia!
Adelia who?
Adelia the cards and
we'll play poker!

Knock, knock.
Who's there?
Alexia!
Alexia who?
Alexia again to open
this door!

Knock, knock.
Who's there?
Alfalfa!
Alfalfa who?
Alfalfa you, if you give me a kiss!

Knock, knock.
Who's there?
Alma!
Alma who?
Alma not going to tell you!

Knock, knock.
Who's there?
Dwayne.
Dwayne who?

Dwayne the bathtub,
I'm dwowning!

Knock, knock.
Who's there?
Althea!
Althea who?
Althea later, alligator!

Knock, knock.
Who's there?
Amahl!
Amahl who?
Amahl shook up!

Knock, knock.
Who's there?
Ammonia!
Ammonia who?
Ammonia little kid!

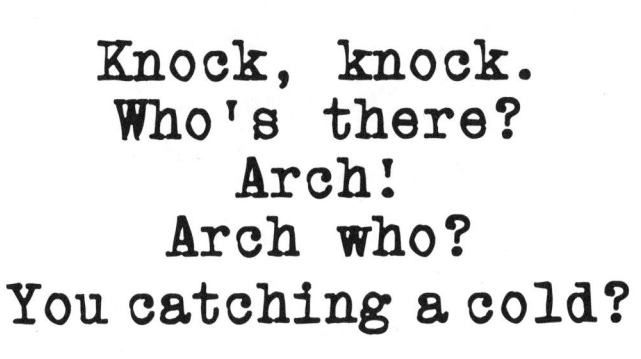

Knock, knock.
Who's there?
Arch!
Arch who?
You catching a cold?

Knock, knock.
Who's there?
Banana.
Banana who?
Knock, knock.
Who's there?
Banana.
Banana who?
Knock, knock.
Who's there?
Orange.
Orange who?
Orange you glad I didn't say banana?

Knock, knock.
Who's there?
Beets!
Beets who?

Beets me!

Knock, knock.
Who's there?
Gestapo.
Gestapo who?

Ve ask ze questions here!

Knock, knock.
Who's there?
Betty!
Betty who?
Betty ya don't know who this is!

Knock, knock.
Who's there?
Butch!
Butch who?
Butch your arms around me!

KNOCK, KNOCK.
WHO'S THERE?
WHO?
WHO WHO?

SORRY, I MUST'VE GOT THE WRONG HOUSE! YOU'RE AN OWL!

Knock, knock.
Who's there?
Candice!
Candice who?
Candice get any better?

Knock, knock.
Who's there?
Cynthia!
Cynthia who?
Cynthia you been away
I missed you!

Knock, knock.
Who's there?
Justin.
Justin who?
Justin old knock-knock joke.

Knock, knock.
Who's there?
Dawn!
Dawn who?
Dawn leave me out here
in the cold!

Knock, knock.
Who's there?
Donovan!
Donovan who?
Donovan know my name!

Knock, knock.
Who's there?
Donna!
Donna who?
Donna sit under an apple tree
with anyone but me!

Knock, knock.
Who's there?
Dozen!
Dozen who?
Dozen anyone ever answer the door?

Knock, knock.
Who's there?
Elizabeth!
Elizabeth who?
Elizabeth of knowledge is
a dangerous thing!

KNOCK, KNOCK.
WHO'S THERE?
ROACH.
ROACH WHO?

ROACH YOU A LETTER. DID YOU GET IT?

Knock, knock.
Who's there?
Ella!
Ella who?
Ella-vator. Doesn't that give you a lift!

Knock, knock.
Who's there?
Emma!
Emma who?
Emma bit cold out here, can you let me in?

Knock, knock.
Who's there?
Europe!
Europe who?
Europe'ning the door too slow, come on!

Knock, knock.
Who's there?
Felix!
Felix who?
Felix my ice cream, I'll lick his!

Knock, knock.
Who's there?
Icy.
Icy who?

I see your underwear!

Knock, knock.
Who's there?
Izzy!
Izzy who?
Izzy come, Izzy go!

Knock, knock.
Who's there?
Juliet!
Juliet who!
Juliet me in or not!

KNOCK, KNOCK.
WHO'S THERE?
HANDSOME!
HANDSOME WHO?
HANDSOME FRENCH FRIES THROUGH THE KEYHOLE AND I'LL TELL YOU MORE!

Knock, knock.
Who's there?
Harriet!
Harriet who?
Harriet up and answer
this door!

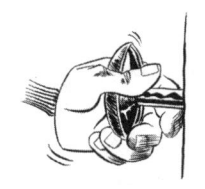

Knock, knock.
Who's there?
Howard!
Howard who?
Howard can it be to guess
a knock-knock joke?

Knock, knock.
Who's there?
Ivana.
Ivana who?

Ivana vash your vindows!

Knock, knock.
Who's there?
Isadore!
Isadore who?
Isadore locked? I can't get in!

Knock, knock.
Who's there?
Isaiah!
Isaiah who?
Isaiah nothing till you open this door!

Knock, knock.
Who's there?
Jewel!
Jewel who?
Jewel know if you open the door!

Knock, knock.
Who's there?
Julie!
Julie who!
Julie your door unlocked?

Knock, knock.
Who's there?
Juicy!
Juicy who?
Juicy what I just saw?

Knock, knock.
Who's there?
Koch!
Koch who?
Koch in the act!

Knock, knock.
Who's there?
Kentucky!
Kentucky who?
Kentucky too well, have a sore throat!

Knock, knock.
Who's there?
Lion!
Lion who?
Lion down on the job again!

Knock, knock.
Who's there?
Werewolf.
Werewolf who?

We're wolfing down Christmas dinner.

Knock, knock.
Who's there?
Midas!
Midas who?
Midas well open the door!

Knock, knock.
Who's there?
Missouri!
Missouri who?
Missouri loves company!

Knock, knock.
Who's there?
Minerva!
Minerva who?
Minerva-s wreck from all
these questions!

Knock, knock.
Who's there?
Olive!
Olive who?
Olive none of your lip!

KNOCK, KNOCK.
WHO'S THERE?
HALLIE!
HALLIE WHO?

HALLIE-TOSIS, YOUR BREATH STINKS!

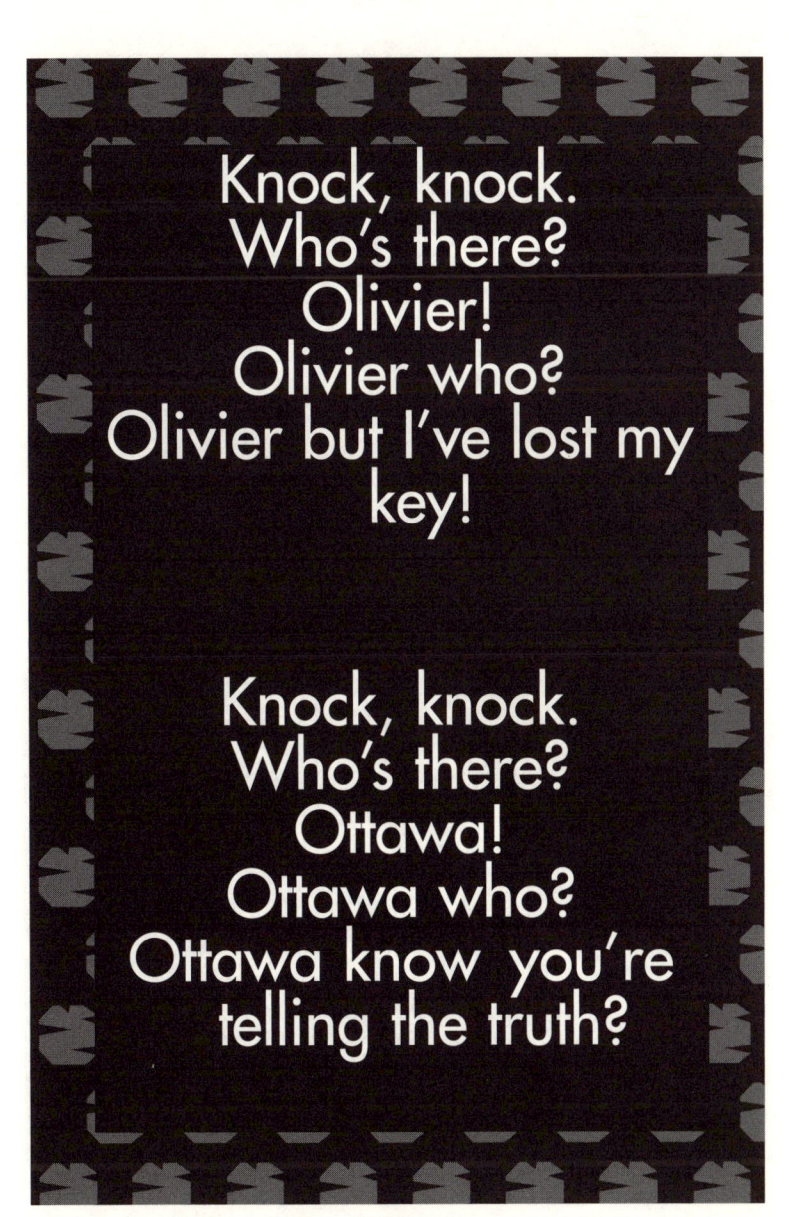

Knock, knock.
Who's there?
Olivier!
Olivier who?
Olivier but I've lost my key!

Knock, knock.
Who's there?
Ottawa!
Ottawa who?
Ottawa know you're telling the truth?

KNOCK, KNOCK.
WHO'S THERE?
SARA!
SARA WHO?
SARA 'NOTHER WAY IN?

KNOCK, KNOCK.
WHO'S THERE?
PASTURE!
PASTURE WHO?
PASTURE BEDTIME, ISN'T IT?

Knock, knock.
Who's there?
Owen!
Owen who?
Owen you open this door, I'm going to give you such a roasting!

Knock, knock.
Who's there?
Rufus!
Rufus who?
Rufus leaking and I'm getting wet!

Knock, knock.
Who's there?
Sacha!
Sacha who?
Sacha fuss, just because I knocked on your door!

Knock, knock.
Who's there?
Nobel.
Nobel who?
No bell, that's why I knocked!

Knock, knock.
Who's there?
Bjorn.
Bjorn who?

Bjorn with a silver spoon in his mouth.

Knock, knock.
Who's there?
Sicily!
Sicily who?
Sicily question!

Knock, knock.
Who's there?
Spain!
Spain who?
Spain to have to keep knocking on this door!

Knock, knock.
Who's there?
Spider!
Spider who?
Spider what everyone says, I like you!

Knock, knock.
Who's there?
Thelonius!
Thelonius who?
Thelonius kid in town!

KNOCK, KNOCK.
WHO'S THERE?
OLIVE.
OLIVE WHO?

OLIVE YOU!

Knock, knock.
Who's there?
Turnip!
Turnip who?
Turnip the heat, it's cold in here!

Knock, knock.
Who's there?
Aida!
Aido who?
Aida lot of sweets and now I've got a tummy ache!

Knock, knock.
Who's there?
Abbott!
Abbott who?
Abbott time you answered the door!

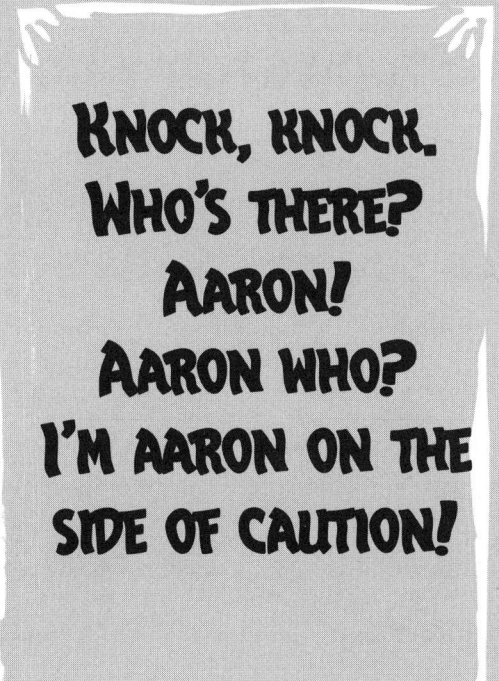

Knock, knock.
Who's there?
Aaron!
Aaron who?
I'm Aaron on the side of caution!

Knock, knock.
Who's there?
Stopwatch!
Stopwatch who?

Stopwatch you're doing
and answer the door!

Knock, knock.
Who's there?
Cass!
Cass who?

Cass more flies
with honey than
vinegar.

Knock, knock.
Who's there?
Justice!
Justice who?
Justice as I thought, no one home!

Knock, knock.
Who's there?
Iowa.
Iowa who?
Iowa lot of money.

Knock, knock.
Who's there?
Albert!
Albert who?
Albert you don't know
who this is!

Knock, knock.
Who's there?
Al.
Al who?
Al give you a kiss if you
open this door!

Knock, knock.
Who's there?
Aladdin!
Aladdin who?

Aladdin the street wants
a word with you!

KNOCK, KNOCK.
WHO'S THERE?
JUSSI!
JUSSI WHO?
JUSSI FRUIT!

KNOCK, KNOCK.
WHO'S THERE?
JUPITER!
JUPITER WHO?
JUPITER FLY IN MY SOUP?

Knock, knock.
Who's there?
Murray.
Murray who?
Murray Christmas!

Knock, knock.
Who's there?
Sheik.
Sheik who?
Sheik and you will find.

Knock, knock.
Who's there?
Didjeridoo.
Didjeridoo who?
Did you redo your homework?

Knock, knock.
Who's there?
Minnie.
Minnie who?
Minnie have tried and many have failed.

Knock, knock.
Who's there?
Elephants.
Elephants who?

Elephants-gerald!

Knock, knock.
Who's there?
Alaska!
Alaska who?
Alaska my friend the question then!

Knock, knock.
Who's there?
Juno!
Juno who?
Juno what time it is?

Knock, knock.
Who's there?
Acid!
Acid who?

Acid down and be quiet!

**Knock, knock.
Who's there?
Ben.
Ben who?**

Ben missing you!

Knock, knock.
Who's there?
Abby.
Abby who?

Abby C D E F G...

Knock, knock.
Who's there?
Earl.
Earl who?

Earl be glad to tell you when you open the door!

Knock, knock.
Who's there?
Ears!
Ears who?
Ears some more knock-knock jokes for you!

Knock, knock.
Who's there?
Huron.
Huron who?
Huron my mind.

Knock, knock.
Who's there?
Howl.
Howl who?
Howl you know unless you open the door?

Knock, knock.
Who's there?
Cows.
Cows who?
Cows don't who. They moo.

Knock, knock.
Who's there?
Catch.
Catch who?
Bless you.

Knock, knock.
Who's there?
Cattle.
Cattle who?
Cattle purr if you give it milk.

Knock, knock.
Who's there?
Lass.
Lass who?
That's what cowboys use, isn't it?

Knock, knock.
Who's there?
Cyrus.
Cyrus who?
Cyrus-ly, what's with the knock-knock jokes?

Knock, knock!
Who's there?
Cargo.

Cargo who?
Cargo beep beep.

Knock, knock.
Who's there?
Abyssinia!
Abyssinia who?
Abyssinia when I get back!

Knock, knock.
Who's there?
Yule.
Yule who?
Yule never know!

Knock, knock.

Who's there?

Adore!

Adore who?

Adore stands between us, open up!

Knock, knock.
Who's there?
Rice.
Rice who?
Rice and shine!

Knock, knock.
Who's there?
Allison!
Allison who?
Allison to you if you'll listen to me!

Knock, knock.
Who's there?
Acute!
Acute who?

Acute little boy!

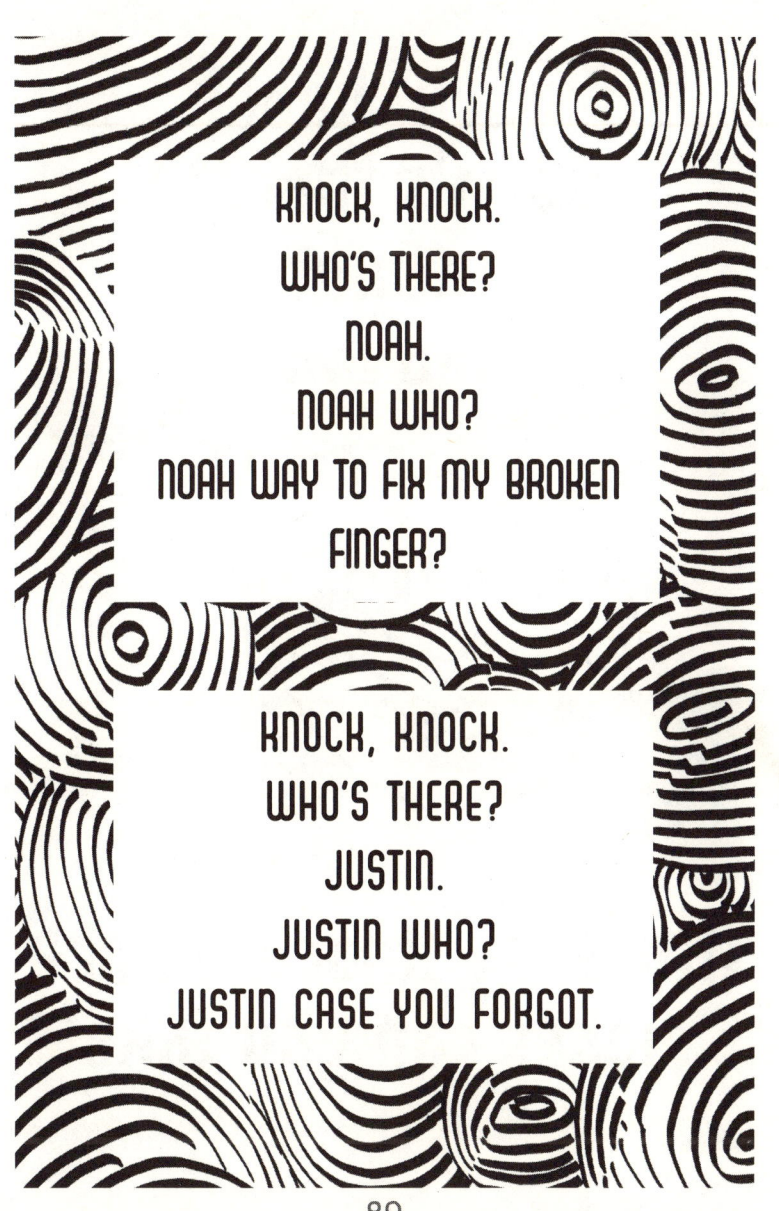

KNOCK, KNOCK.
WHO'S THERE?
NOAH.
NOAH WHO?
NOAH WAY TO FIX MY BROKEN FINGER?

KNOCK, KNOCK.
WHO'S THERE?
JUSTIN.
JUSTIN WHO?
JUSTIN CASE YOU FORGOT.

Knock, knock.
Who's there?
Alma!
Alma who?

Alma-ny Knock-knock jokes can you take!

KNOCK, KNOCK.
WHO'S THERE?
HOWARD.
HOWARD WHO?
HOWARD WE GONNA GET YOU
TO EAT YOUR VEGETABLES?

KNOCK, KNOCK.
WHO'S THERE?
BOTTOMLESS.
BOTTOMLESS WHO?
BOTTOMLESS-ONS IN TENNIS
FOR HIS BIRTHDAY.

Knock, knock.
Who's there?
Amanda!
Amanda who?
Amanda fix the television!

Knock, knock.
Who's there?
Ann!
Ann who?
Ann-onymous!

Knock, knock.
Who's there?
Aretha!
Aretha who?
Aretha flowers!

Knock, knock.
Who's there?
Arthur!
Arthur who!
Arthur any dogs in your house?

Knock, knock.
Who's there?
Mary lee.
Mary lee who?
Mary lee we roll along.

Knock, knock.
Who's there?
Tom Sawyer.
Tom Sawyer who?
Tom Sawyer cheating
off his test.

Knock, knock.
Who's there?
Disaster!
Disaster who?
Disaster be my lucky day.

Knock, knock.
Who's there?
Armenia!
Armenia who?
Armenia every word
I say!

Knock, knock.
Who's there?
Apple!
Apple who?

Apple your hair if you don't let me in!

Knock, knock.
Who's there?
Thistle.
Thistle who?
Thistle make you feel better.

Knock, knock.
Who's there?
Axel!
Axel who?
Axeldental Tourist!

Knock, knock!
Who's there?
Iran.
Iran who?
Iran all the way home.

Knock, knock.
Who's there?
Hugo.
Hugo who?
Hugo first...I'm scared.

Knock, knock.
Who's there?
Kanga!
Kanga who?
No, Kangaroo!

Knock, knock.
Who's there?
Centipede.
Centipede who?

Centipede on the Christmas tree.

Knock, knock.
Who's there?
Shore.
Shore who?
Shore would like it if you bought me some pizza.

Knock, knock.
Who's there?
Oliver.
Oliver who?
Oliver time was taken up doing invisibility experiments.

Will you remember me in a week?
Yes.
How about in 5 years?
Yes.
Knock, knock.
Who's there?
You forgot me already!

Knock, knock.
Who's there?
Joe.
Joe who?
Joe Mama!

Knock, knock.
Who's there?
Heart!
Heart who?
Heart to hear you, speak louder!

Knock, knock.
Who's there?
Oscar.
Oscar who?
Oscar if she knows how to get to the library.

Knock, knock.
Who's there?
Armageddon!
Armageddon who?

Armageddon out of here!

KNOCK, KNOCK.
WHO'S THERE?
HEAVEN!
HEAVEN WHO?
HEAVEN SEEN YOU IN AGES!

KNOCK, KNOCK.
WHO'S THERE?
NUNYA.
NUNYA WHO?
NUNYA BUSINESS.

KNOCK, KNOCK.
WHO'S THERE?
BEN.
BEN WHO?
BEN DOVER.

KNOCK, KNOCK.
WHO'S THERE?
IMA.
IMA WHO?
WHAT'S A WHO?

**Knock, knock.
Who's there?
Avocado!
Avocado who?**

Avocado cold!

Knock, knock.
Who's there?
Punch!
Punch who?
Not me—I just got here!

Knock, knock.
Who's there?
Orange juice!
Orange juice who?
Orange juice going to talk to me?

Knock, knock.
Who's there?
Kent.
Kent who?

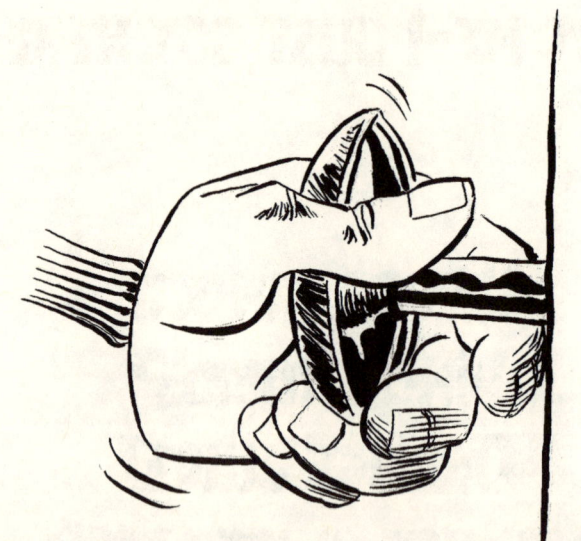

Kent you tell by my voice?

knock, knock.
Who's there?
Sarah.
Sarah who?

Sarah phone I could use?

Knock, knock.
Who's there?
Viper.
Viper who?

Viper your nose!

Knock, knock.
Who's there?
Maiden.
Maiden who?
Maiden America!

Knock, knock.
Who's there?
Sid.
Sid who
Sid down and be quiet.

Knock, knock.
Who's there?
Avenue!
Avenue who?
Avenue heard the good news?

Knock, knock.
Who's there?
Amy!
Amy who?
Amy fraid I've forgotten!

Knock, knock.
Who's there?
Dummy!
Dummy who?
Dummy a favor and go away!

Knock, knock.
Who's there?
Ice cream!
Ice cream who?
Ice cream if you don't let me in!

Knock, knock.
Who's there?
Oily.
Oily who?
Oily to bed, oily to rise.

Knock, knock.
Who's there?
Cheese!
Cheese who?
Cheese! Just open the door and let me in!

Knock, knock.
Who's there?
Heidi!
Heidi who?

Heidi-clare war on you!

Knock, knock.
Who's there?
Bless!
Bless who?
I didn't sneeze!

Knock, knock.
Who's there?
Trigger.
Trigger who?
Trigger treat?

Knock, knock.
Who's there?
Tank.
Tank who?
You're welcome!

Knock, knock.
Who's there?
Hawaii.
Hawaii who?
I'm fine, Hawaii you?

Knock, knock.
Who's there?
Pea.
Pea who?

Pea you, you smell!

Knock, knock.
Who's there?
Water!
Water who?
Water way to answer the door!

Knock, knock.
Who's there?
Figs!
Figs who?
Figs the doorbell, it's broken.

Knock, knock.
Whos there?
Dismay!
Dismay who?
Dismay be a joke but it doesn't make me laugh!

Knock, knock.
Whos there?
Dozen!
Dozen who?
Dozen anyone live here anymore?

Knock, knock.
Who's there?
Helena!
Helena who?

Helena hand basket.

Knock, knock.
Who's there?
Waddle!
Waddle who?
Waddle you give me if I go away?

Knock, knock.
Who's there?
Wicked!
Wicked who?
Wicked go for long walks together!

Knock, knock.
Who's there?
Atlas!
Atlas?
Atlas it's the weekend!

Knock, knock.
Who's there?
Atomic!
Atomic who?
Atomic ache!

Knock, knock.
Who's there?
Axl!
Axl who?
Axl me nicely and I might just tell you!

Knock, knock.
Who's there?
Anita!
Anita who?
Anita you like I need a hole in the head!

Knock, knock.
Who's there?
Alda!
Alda who?
Alda time you knew
who it was!

Knock, knock.
Who's there?
Ida.
Ida who?
Ida her face. She's too
ugly!

Knock, knock.
Who's there?
Deanna.
Deanna who?

Deanna-mals are restless,
open the door.

KNOCK, KNOCK.
WHO'S THERE?
BABY OWL!
BABY OWL WHO?
BABY OWL SEE YOU LATER, MAYBE I WON'T!

Knock, knock.
Who's there?
Theodore.
Theodore who?
Theodore bell doesn't work...let me in.

Knock, knock.
Who's there?
Electrician.
Electrician who?
Here to fix the doorbell, ma'am.

Knock, knock.
Who's there?
Ice cream soda.
Ice cream soda who?
Ice cream soda people can hear me.

Knock, knock.
Who's there?
Norma Lee.
Norma Lee who?
Norma Lee I don't knock on doors.

KNOCK, KNOCK.
WHO'S THERE?
NORMAN.
NORMAN WHO?
NORMAN IS AN ISLAND.

KNOCK, KNOCK.
WHO'S THERE?
CARRIE.
CARRIE WHO?
CARRIE ME HOME, MY FEET ARE TIRED!

KNOCK, KNOCK.
WHO'S THERE?
TRIO.
TRIO WHO?
TRIO'CLOCK IN THE MORNING!

KNOCK, KNOCK.
WHO'S THERE?
JUAN.
JUAN WHO?
JUAN OF YOUR FRIENDS.

Knock, knock.
Who's there?
Will.
Will who?

Will you open the door already?

Knock, knock.
Who's there?
Wanda.
Wanda who?

Wanda door opens,
I'll stop knocking.

Knock, knock.
Who's there?
Doris.
Doris who?

Doris locked, I'm coming in through the window!

Knock, knock.
Who's there?
Barry.
Barry who?
Barry nice to see you!

Knock, knock.
Who's there?
Kenya.
Kenya who?
Kenya shut up?

Knock, knock.
Who's there?
José.
José who?
José can you see by the dawn's early light?

Knock, knock.
Who's there?
Carmen.
Carmen who?
Carmen get it!

Knock, knock.
Who's there?
Tell.
Tell who?
Don't tell anybody it's
a secret.

Knock, knock.
Who's there?
Europe.
Europe who?
Europe the creek without
a paddle.

Knock, knock.
Who's there?
Hit.
Hit who?
I don't care, just don't hit me!

Knock, knock.
Who's there?
You.
You who?
You hoo! Are you letting
me in?

Knock, knock.
Who's there?
Ken.
Ken who?

Ken you come out and play?

Knock, knock.
Who's there?
Teresa.
Teresa who?
Teresa are tall and green.

Knock, knock.
Who's there?
Ezra.
Ezra who?
Ezra no hope for me in this world!

Knock, knock.
Who's there?
Pear.
Pear who?
Pear–haps I'll see you later.

Knock, knock.
Who's there?
Buster.
Buster who?
Buster gut!

Knock, knock.
Who's there?
Ben.
Ben who?
Ben knocking on the door all afternoon!

Knock, knock.
Who's there?
Closure.
Closure who?
Closure mouth when you're eating!

Knock, knock.
Who's there?
Hand.
Hand who?

Hand over your wallet, this is a stick up!

Knock, knock.
Who's there?
Daisy.
Daisy who?
Daisy that you are in, but I don't believe them.

Knock, knock.
Who's there?
Venice.
Venice who?
Venice your mother coming?

Knock, knock.
Who's there?
Hive.
Hive who?
Hive a crush on you!

Knock, knock.
Who's there?
Beezer.
Beezer who?
Beezer black and yellow and make honey.

Knock, knock.
Who's there?
Lucretia.
Lucretia who?

Lucretia from the Black Lagoon!

Knock, knock.
Who's there?
Dime
Dime who?
Dime to tell another
knock-knock joke!

Knock, knock?
Who's there?
Moppet.
Moppet who?
Moppet up before it gets sticky.

Knock, knock.
Who's there?
Sam.
Sam who?
Sam person who knocked on the door last time!

Knock, knock.
Who's there?
Luke.
Luke who?
Luke through the keyhole and you'll see...

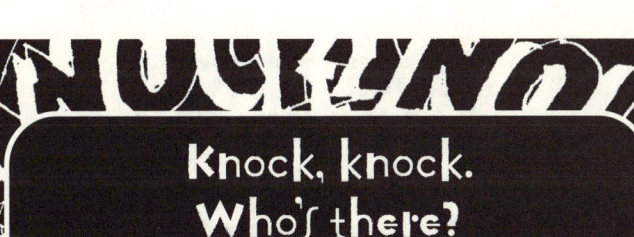

Knock, knock.
Who's there?
Nadia.
Nadia who?
Just Nadia head if you understand what I'm saying.

Knock, knock.
Who's there?
Nuisance.
Nuisance who?
What's nuisance yesterday?

KNOCK, KNOCK.
WHOS THERE?
CANOE.
CANOE WHO?

CANOE YOU LEND ME SOME MONEY?

Knock, knock.
Who's there?
I don't know.
I don't know who?
I told you I don't know. Why don't you believe me?

Knock, knock.
Who's there?
Lionel.
Lionel who?
Lionel get you nowhere, better tell the truth!

Knock, knock.
Who's there?
Butter!
Butter who?

Butter open quick, I have to go to the bathroom!

Knock, knock.
Who's there?
Teddy.
Teddy who?
Teddy is the beginning of the rest of your life!

Knock, knock.
Who's there?
Odysseus!
Odysseus who?
Odysseus the last straw!

KNOCK, KNOCK.
WHO'S THERE?
LISA.
LISA WHO?
LISA YOU CAN DO IS LET ME IN!

KNOCK, KNOCK.
WHO'S THERE?
MAINE.
MAINE WHO?
MAINE I COME IN NOW PLEASE?

KNOCK, KNOCK.
WHO'S THERE?
TELLY.
TELLY WHO?
TELLY YOUR FRIEND TO COME OUT.

KNOCK, KNOCK.
WHO'S THERE?
FANNY.
FANNY WHO?
FANNY BODY CALLS, I'M OUT.

Knock, knock.
Who's there?
Tennis.
Tennis who?
Tennis five plus five.

Knock, knock.
Who's there?
Mabel.
Mabel who?
Mabel doesn't ring either...

Knock, knock.
Who's there?
Ina.
Ina who?

Ina minute I'm going to knock this door down!

Knock, knock.
Who's there?
Scold.
Scold who?
Scold outside.

Knock, knock.
Who's there?
Emile.
Emile who?
Emile fit for a king!

Knock, knock.
Who's there?
Lima bean.
Lima bean who?
Lima bean too busy
to call.

Knock, knock.
Who's there?
Ivan.
Ivan who?
Ivan new hat. Do you
like it?

Knock, knock.
Who's there?
Eyesore.
Eyesore who?
Eyesore do like you!

Knock, knock.
Who's there?
Hal.
Hal who?
Hal who to you too!

Knock, knock.
Who's there?
Diploma!
Diploma who?

Diploma to fix the leak!

Knock, knock.
Who's there?
Kathy.
Kathy who?
Kathy you again?

Knock, knock.
Who's there?
Gene.
Gene who?
Gene-e-alogy.

Knock, knock.
Who's there?
Gwen.
Gwen who?
Gwen fishing, want to come?

Knock, knock.
Who's there?
Iguana.
Iguana who?
Iguana hold your hand.

Knock, knock.
Who's there?
Rita.
Rita who?
Rita book instead of reading these dumb knock-knock jokes!

Knock, knock.
Who's there?
Dishes.
Dishes who?
Dishes me. Who ish you?

Knock, knock.
Who's there?
Eileen.
Eileen who?
Eileen down to tie my shoe.

Knock, knock.
Who's there?
Thistle.
Thistle who?
Thistle have to hold you until dinner's ready.

Knock, knock.
Who's there?
Hammond.
Hammond who?
Hammond eggs for breakfast.

Knock, knock.
Who's there?
Zany.
Zany who?
Zany body home?

Knock, knock.
Who's there?
Tamara.
Tamara who?

Tamara the world!

Knock, knock.
Who's there?
Ray.
Ray who?

Ray-ning cats and dogs, let me in!

Knock, knock.
Who's there?
Ears!
Ears who?
Ears some more knock-knock jokes for you!

Knock, knock.
Who's there?
Roxanne.
Roxanne who?
Roxanne pebbles are in my shoes.

Knock, knock.
Who's there?
Hominy.
Hominy who?
Hominy times do I have to knock before you'll open the door?

Knock, knock.
Who's there?
Ears!
Ears who?
Ears looking at you!

Knock, knock.
Who's there?
Randy.
Randy who?

Randy mile in less than five minutes!

Knock, knock.
Who's there?
Island.
Island who?

Island on your roof with my parachute.

Knock, knock.
Who's there?
Diesel!
Diesel who?
Diesel teach me to go knocking around on doors.

Knock, knock.
Who's there?
Diesel!
Diesel who?
Diesel be your bag on the step I suppose?

Knock, knock.
Who's there?
Egg!
Egg who?
Eggstremely cold waiting for you to open the door!

Knock, knock.
Who's there?
Debussy.
Debussy who?
Debussy C. Fields!

Knock, knock.
Who's there?
Dewey.
Dewey who?
Dewey have to do
these jokes all night?

Knock, knock.
Who's there?
Agatha.
Agatha who?
Agatha blues!

Knock, knock.
Who's there?
Luke.
Luke who?
Luke for the silver lining...

Knock, knock.
Who's there?
Disk!
Disk who?
Disk is a recording, please leave your message after the beep!

Knock, knock.
Who's there?
Andrew!
Andrew who?

Andrew all over the wall, and boy is she in big trouble!

Knock, knock.
Who's there?
Dozen!
Dozen who?
Dozen anybody want
to play with me?

Knock, knock.
Irish.
Irish who?
Irish you a merry
Christmas!

Knock, knock.
Who's there?
Amy Vaughan.
Amy Vaughan who?
Ready...Amy...Vaughan,
two, three, FIRE!

Knock, knock.
Who's there?
I'm a Green.
I'm a Green who?
I'm agree'n with you.

Knock, knock.
Who's there?
Disguise!
Disguise who?

Disguise the limit!

Knock, knock.
Who's there?
How.
How who?
Shh! You'll wake up the neighbors.

Knock, knock.
Who's there?
Sofa!
Sofa who?
Sofa...so good!

Knock, knock.
Who's there?
Why.
Why who?
Gee you sure seem excited today.

Knock, knock.
Who's there?
Tito.
Tito who?
Do, re, mi, fa, so, la, tito.

Knock, knock.
Who's there?
Dishes!
Dishes who?
Dishes the police!

Knock, knock.
Who's there?
Dishes!
Dishes who?
Dishes a very bad joke!

Knock, knock.
Who's there?
Karma.
Karma who?
Can I borrow the kar, ma?

Knock, knock.
Who's there?
Bertha.
Bertha who?
Bertha painful thing, ain't it?

Knock, knock.
Who's there?
Thesis.
Thesis who?
Thesis a very funny joke!

Knock, knock.
Who's there?
Utah.
Utah who?
Utah a putty tat! You did!
You did!

Knock, knock.
Who's there?
Pencil.
Pencil who?
Pencil fall down if you don't wear a belt!

Knock, knock.
Who's there?
Gope.
Gope who?
I don't have to.

Knock, knock.
Who's there?
Raoul.
Raoul who?

Raoul with the punches!

Knock, knock!
Who's there?
Olivia!
Olivia who?
Olivia in Birmingham. Where do you livia?

Knock, knock.
Who's there?
Jest.
Jest who?
Jest one of those things.

Knock, knock.
Who's there?
Oswald.
Oswald who?
Oswald my gum!

Knock, knock.
Who's there?
Panther.
Panther who?
Panther no panth, I'm going thwimming!

Knock, knock.
Who's there?
Dragon!
Dragon who?

Dragon your feet again!

Knock, knock.
Who's there?
Toodle?
Toodle who?
Bye bye.

Knock, knock.
Who's there?
Desdemona.
Desdemona who?
Desdemona Lisa hanging on the museum wall.

Knock, knock.
Who's there?
Evan.
Evan who?
Evan only knows.

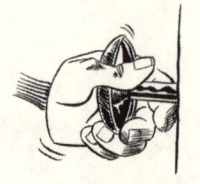

Knock, knock.
Who's there?
Garden.
Garden who?
Garden the treasure.

Knock, knock.
Who's there?
Dude.
Dude who?
Eeewww! U said DooDoo!

Knock, knock.
Who's there?
Ozzy.
Ozzy who?
Ozzy you around.

Knock, knock.
Who's there?
Mae.
Mae who?
Mae be I'll tell you
or Mae be I won't...

Knock, knock.
Who's there?
Waiter.
Waiter who?
Waiter minute while I tie
my shoelaces.

Knock, knock.
Who's there?
Keanu.
Keanu who?
Keanu let me in, it's cold out here!

Knock, knock.
Who's there?
A little girl.
A little girl who?
A little girl who can't reach the doorbell!

Knock, knock.
Who's there?
Gala!
Gala who?
Galafornia here I come!

Knock, knock.
Who's there?
Gary.
Gary who?
Gary on smiling!

Knock, knock.
Who's there?
Auto!
Auto who?

Auto know, but I've forgotten!

Knock, knock.
Who's there?
Unite.
Unite who?

Unite a person, you call him sir afterwards.

Knock, knock.
Who's there?
Gertie.
Gertie who?
Gertie-sy call!

Knock, knock.
Who's there?
Sadie.
Sadie who?
Sadie Pledge of Allegiance!

Knock, knock.
Who's there?
Sally.
Sally who?

Sallybrate the moments of your life!

Knock, knock.
Who's there?
Deesa.
Deesa who?

Deesapear and don't come back!

Knock, knock.
Who's there?
Mikey.
Mikey who?
My key doesn't fit in
my keyhole!

Knock, knock.
Who's there?
Jenny.
Jenny who?
Je need any help?

Knock, knock.
Who's there?
Ghost.
Ghost who?
Go start the show, the crowd's waiting.

Knock, knock.
Who's there?
Ivan.
Ivan who?
I've invested all my money.

Knock, knock.
Who's there?
Hide out.
Hide out who?
Hi doubt you can stop
being annoying.

Knock, knock.
Who's there?
Ivory.
Ivory who?
I've returned to the place of
my birth.

Knock, knock.
Who's there?
Thayer.
Thayer who?

Thayer thorry and I won't throw thisth pie in your face!

Knock, knock.
Who's there?
Seagull.
Seagull who?
See gull, see boy.

Knock, knock.
Who's there?
Hal!
Hal who?
Hallelujah Chorus!

Knock, knock.
Who's there?
Thumb.
Thumb who?
Thumb times I just don't know about you!

Knock, knock.
Who's there?
Jano.
Jano who?
Ja notice how easy it is to get past Security?

Knock, knock.
Who's there?
Minviz.
Minviz who?
'Minvizible. Help!

Knock, knock.
Who's there?
Justice.
Justice who?
Justice once won't you be quiet?

Knock, knock.
Who's there?
Aileen!
Aileen who?

Aileen Dover and fell down!

Knock, knock.
Who's there?
Edible.
Edible who?
Edible-ony sandwich for lunch.

Knock, knock.
Who's there?
Donate.
Donate who?
Doan ate the peas, while Doan's brother ate the carrots.

Knock, knock.
Who's there?
Sheila.
Sheila who?
She loves to play piano.

Knock, knock.
Who's there?
Attitude.
Attitude who?
Added two dimes and
got twenty cents.

Knock, knock.
Who's there?
Alma!
Alma who?

Alma candy's gone!

KNOCK, KNOCK.
WHO'S THERE?
BOTANY.
BOTANY WHO?
BOTANY GOOD JELLYBEANS
LATELY?

KNOCK, KNOCK.
WHO'S THERE?
DENY.
DENY WHO?
DENIGHT IS WHEN DESTARS
SHINE.

Knock, knock.
Who's there?
Wanda.
Wanda who?
Wanda why you keep forgetting who I am.

Knock, knock.
Who's there?
Sarah.
Sarah who?
Sarah nuther piece of pie?

Knock, knock.
Who's there?
Winner.
Winner who?
Winner you gonna stop being so annoying?

Knock, knock.
Who's there?
Arthur.
Arthur who?
Arthur more cookies in the jar?

Knock, knock.
Who's there?
Ivan.
Ivan who?

Ivan infectious disease.

Knock, knock.
Who's there?
Who.
Who who?
What... is there an owl in here?

Knock, knock.
Who's there?
Boil.
Boil who?
Cannibal!

Knock, knock.
Who's there?
Ada!
Ada who?

Ada burger for lunch!

Knock, knock.
Who's there?
Howard.
Howard who?
Howard we gonna get you to eat your vegetables?

Knock, knock.
Who's there?
Macho.
Macho who?
Macho-do about nothing!

Knock, knock.
Who's there?
Consumption.
Consumption who?
Consumption be done about all these bad knock-knock jokes?

Knock, knock.
Who's there?
Alex.
Alex who?
Al explain later.

Knock, knock.
Who's there?
Snow.
Snow who?
Snow one here but me.

Knock, knock.
Who's there?
Maura.
Maura who?
Maura or less.

KNOCK, KNOCK.
WHO'S THERE?
STATUE.
STATUE WHO?
STATUE OR SOMEONE ELSE?

KNOCK, KNOCK.
WHO'S THERE?
NONA.
NONA WHO?
NONA YOUR BUSINESS.

Knock, knock.
Who's there?
Al.
Al who?

Al go home if you're not nice to me!

Knock, knock.
Who's there?
Halibut!
Halibut who?
Halibut a kiss, sweetheart!

Knock, knock.
Who's there?
Hardy!
Hardy who?
Hardy ha ha!

Knock, knock.
Who's there?
Genoa.
Genoa who?
Genoa good teacher?

Knock, knock.
Who's there?
Germaine.
Germaine who?
Germaine you don't recognize me?

Knock, knock.
Who's there?
Halifax!
Halifax who?

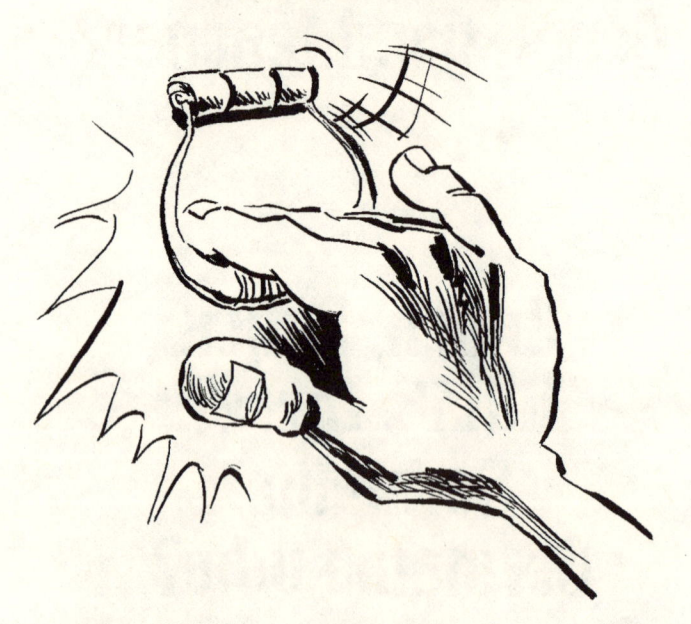

Halifax you if you fax me!

Knock, knock.
Who's there?
Tarzan.
Tarzan who?

Tarzan Stripes Forever!

Knock, knock.
Who's there?
Harmony!
Harmony who?
Harmony knock-knock jokes do you expect me to know?

Knock, knock.
Who's there?
Police.
Police who?
Police let us in; it's cold out here.

KNOCK, KNOCK.
WHO'S THERE?
HANNAH!
HANNAH WHO?
HANNAH PARTRIDGE IN A PEAR TREE!

KNOCK, KNOCK.
WHO'S THERE?
HARLOW!
HARLOW WHO?
HARLOW WILL YOU GO?

Knock, knock.
Who's there?
Toreador.
Toreador who?

Open up or I'll toreador down!

KNOCK, KNOCK!
WHO'S THERE?
I LOVE.
I LOVE WHO?
I DON'T KNOW, YOU TELL ME!

KNOCK, KNOCK!
WHO'S THERE?
REED.
REED WHO?
REED BETWEEN THE LINES.

Knock, knock!
Who's there?
Quacker.
Quacker who?
Quacker another bad knock-knock joke and I'm leaving!

Knock, knock!
Who's there?
Utah.
Utah who?
Utah sight, Utah mind.

Knock, knock!
Who's there?
Zippy.
Zippy Who?
Zippy dee-doo-dah, zippy dee hey!

Knock, knock!
Who's there?
Dana.
Dana who?
Dana talk with your mouth full.

Knock, knock.
Who's there?
Formosa.
Formosa who?
Formosa the summer I was away on my holiday.

Knock, knock.
Who's there?
Sherlock.
Sherlock who?
Sherlock your door! Someone could break in...

Knock, knock.
Who's there?
Falafel.
Falafel who?
Falafel off his bike and hurt his knee!

Knock, knock.
Who's there?
Leland.
Leland who?
Leland of the free and the home of the brave!

KNOCK, KNOCK.
WHO'S THERE?
TRUFFLE.
TRUFFLE WHO?
TRUFFLE WITH YOU IS THAT
YOU ARE SO SHY.

KNOCK, KNOCK.
WHO'S THERE?
TRIXIE.
TRIXIE WHO?
TRIXIE COULDN'T DO BECAUSE
HE WAS A BAD MAGICIAN!

Knock, knock.
Who's there?
Aardvark.
Aardvark who?

Aardvark a million miles for one of your smiles!

Knock, knock.
Who's there?
Violet.
Violet who?
Violet the cat out of
the bag.

Knock, knock.
Who's there?
Usher.
Usher who?
Usher wish you would let
me in!

Knock, knock.
Who's there?
Ina.
Ina who?
Ina Claire day, you can see for miles!

Knock, knock.
Who's there?
Norway.
Norway who?
Norway will I leave till you open this door!

Knock, knock.
Who's there?
Thermos.
Thermos who?
Thermos be a better
knock-knock joke than this!

Knock, knock.
Who's there?
Foster.
Foster who?
Foster than a
speeding bullet!

Knock, knock.
Who's there?
Lilli.
Lilli who?
Lilli Brown jug upon
my knee!

Knock, knock.
Who's there?
Imogen.
Imogen who?
Imogen life without
chocolate!

**Knock, knock.
Who's there?
Gouda.
Gouda who?**

**Gouda cheese comes from
happy cows.**

Knock, knock.
Who's there?
Thatcher.
Thatcher who?
Thatcher could get away with it?

Knock, knock.
Who's there?
Bart.
Bart who?
Bart up the wrong tree!

Knock, knock.
Who's there?
Barry.
Barry who?
Barry the treasure where
no one will find it.

Knock, knock.
Who's there?
Blue.
Blue who?
Blue away with the wind!

Knock, knock.
Who's there?
Zubin.
Zubin who?
Zubin eating garlic again?

Knock, knock.
Who's there?
Tara.
Tara who?
Tara-ra boom-de-ay!

Knock, knock.
Who's there?
Vanilla.
Vanilla who?
Vanilla call the doctor?

Knock, knock.
Who's there?
Wade.
Wade who?
Wade up little Susie!

Knock, knock.
Who's there?
Mister.
Mister who?
Mister by an inch!

Knock, knock.
Who's there?
Lenny.
Lenny who?
Lenny in, I'm hungry.

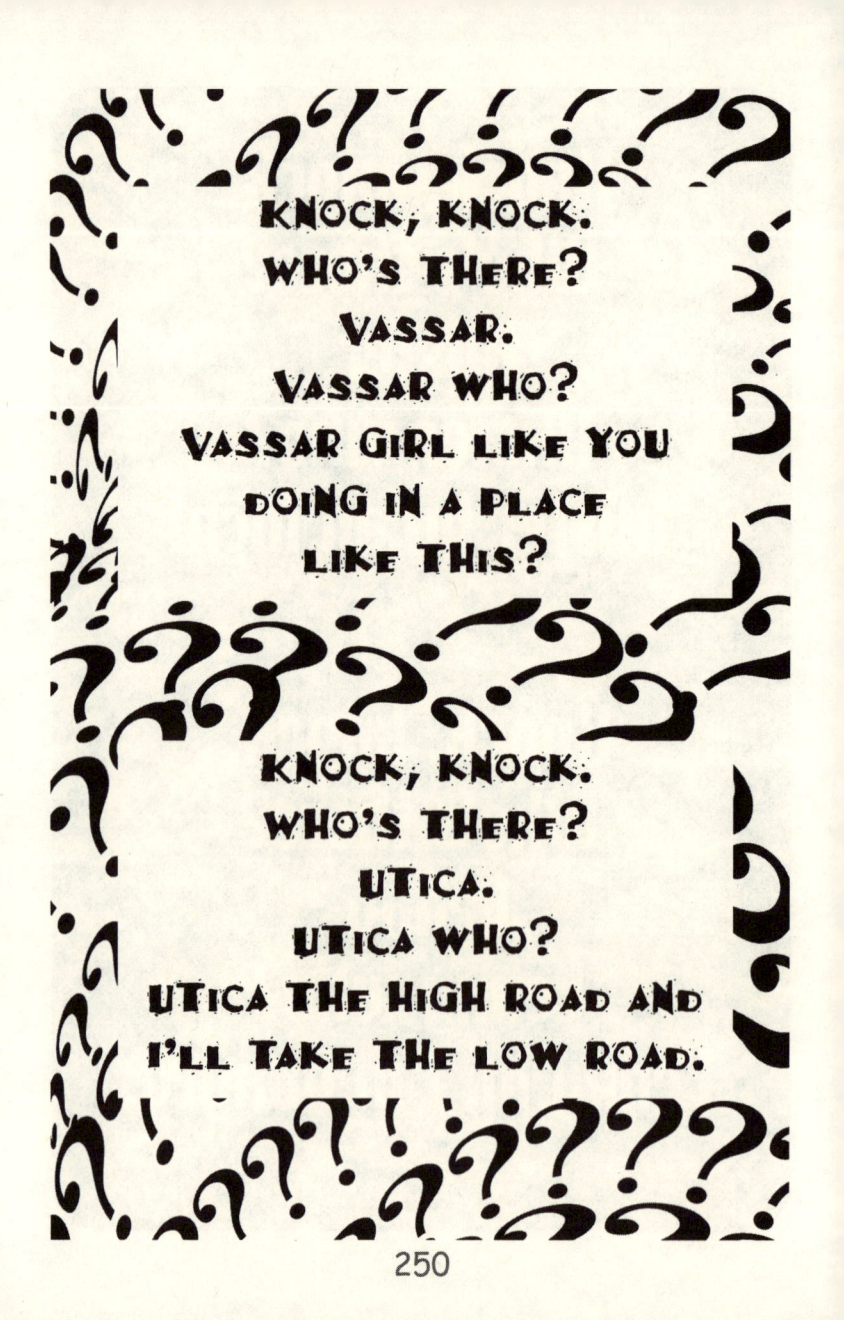

Knock, knock.
Who's there?
Vassar.
Vassar who?
Vassar girl like you
doing in a place
like this?

Knock, knock.
Who's there?
Utica.
Utica who?
Utica the high road and
I'll take the low road.

KNOCK, KNOCK.
WHO'S THERE?
PROFESSOR.
PROFESSOR WHO?

HOW ABOUT YOU GO AND
PROFESSOR YOUR LOVE TONIGHT?

Knock, knock.
Who's there?
Balloon.
Balloon who?
Balloon velvet!

Knock, knock.
Who's there?
Ogre.
Ogre who?
Ogre take a flying leap.

Knock, knock.
Who's there?
Tammy.
Tammy who?
Tammycles' sword!

Knock, knock.
Who's there?
Band.
Band who?
Band in Boston!

KNOCK, KNOCK.
WHO'S THERE?
YURI.
YURI WHO?

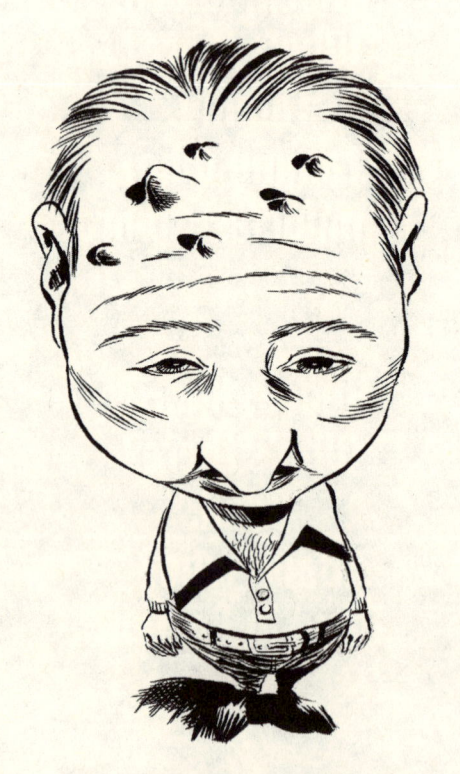

YURI-CEDING HAIRLINE REVEALS YOUR LUMPY HEAD.

Knock, knock.
Who's there?
Yachts.
Yachts who?
Yachts up, doc?!

Knock, knock.
Who's there?
Lionel.
Lionel who?
Lionel bite you if you put your head in its mouth!

Knock, knock.
Who's there?
Yehuda.
Yehuda who?
Yehuda dance all night.

Knock, knock.
Who's there?
Zebulon.
Zebulon who?
Zebulon to me!

Knock, knock.
Who's there?
Mary.
Mary who?

Mary me and we'll live happily ever after.

KNOCK, KNOCK.
WHO'S THERE?
ZONE.
ZONE WHO?
ZONE SHADOW SCARES HIM!

KNOCK, KNOCK.
WHO'S THERE?
ACTOR.
ACTOR WHO?
ACTOR YOU, MY DEAR!

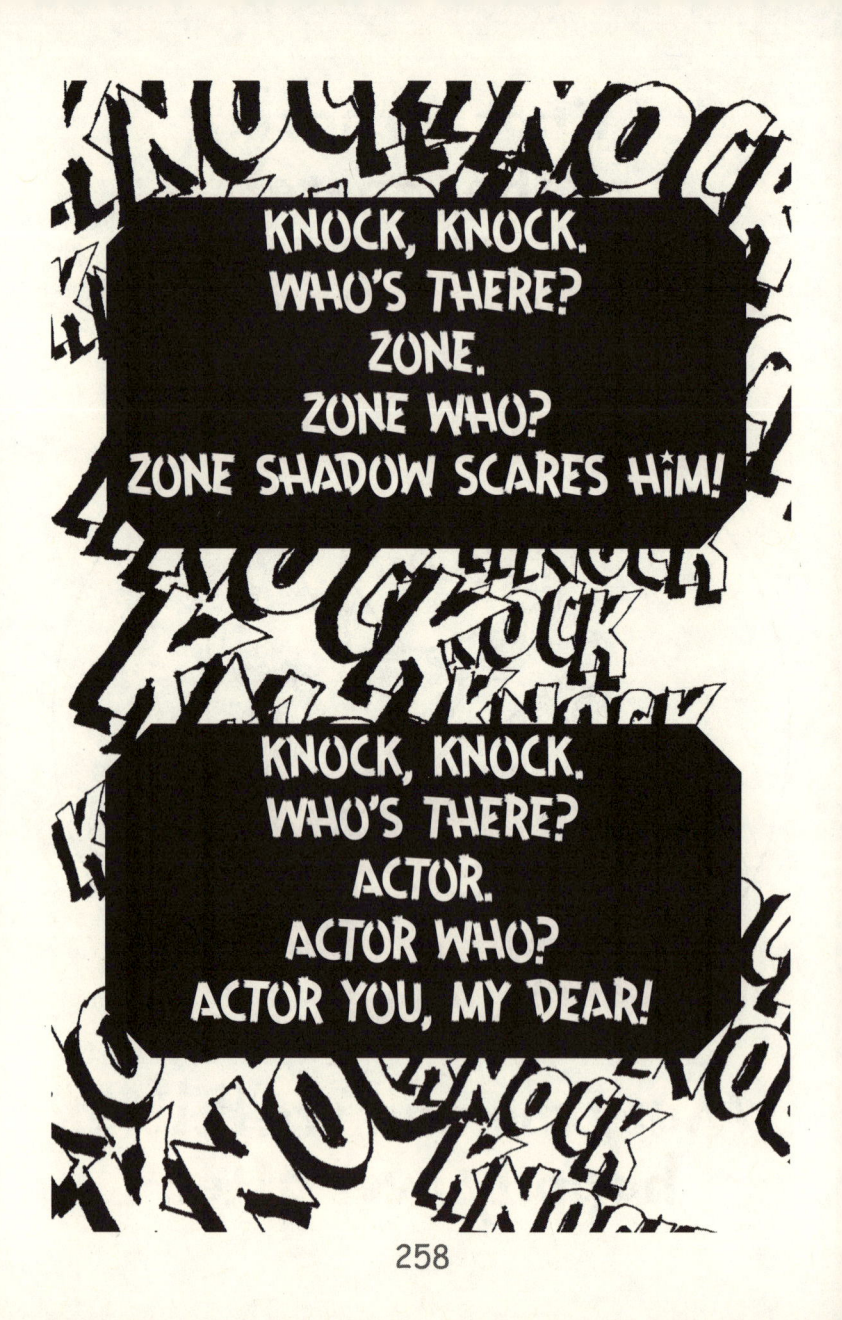

KNOCK, KNOCK.
WHO'S THERE?
RAY.
RAY WHO?
RAY-DERS OF THE LOST ARK.

KNOCK, KNOCK.
WHO'S THERE?
TEX.
TEX WHO?
TEX TWO TO TANGO.

Knock, knock.
Who's there?
Major.
Major who?

Major B. Hindsor when you got spanked!

Knock, knock.
Who's there?
Dakota.
Dakota who?

Dakota is too long in the arms.

KNOCK, KNOCK.
WHO'S THERE?
EURIPEDES.
EURIPEDES WHO?

EURIPEDES PHONEBOOKS IN HALF AND YOU'RE HIRED.

KNOCK, KNOCK.
WHO'S THERE?
LESLIE.
LESLIE WHO?
LESLIE TOWN NOW BEFORE
THEY CATCH US.

KNOCK, KNOCK.
WHO'S THERE?
ED.
ED WHO?
ED-VANCED PAIN MEDICINE.

KNOCK, KNOCK.
WHO'S THERE?
LES.
LES WHO?
LES GO FOR A SWIM!

KNOCK, KNOCK.
WHO'S THERE?
TENNESSEE.
TENNESSEE WHO?
TENNESSEE YOU LATER.

Knock, knock.
Who's there?
Pecan!
Pecan who?

Pecan somebody your own size!

Knock, knock.
Who's there?
Major.
Major who?
Major headache, please gimme aspirin!

Knock, knock.
Who's there?
Reddy.
Reddy who?
Reddy Teddy?

Knock, knock.
Who's there?
Havelock.
Havelock who?
Havelock put on your door!

Knock, knock.
Who's there?
Element.
Element who?
Element to tell you that she can't see you today.

Knock, knock.
Who's there?
Renato.
Renato who?
Renato gas last night?

Knock, knock.
Who's there?
Urchin.
Urchin who?
Urchin is pointy.

Knock, knock.
Who's there?
Bud.
Bud who?
Bud, sweat, 'n tears.

Knock, knock.
Who's there?
Buddha.
Buddha who?
Buddha this slice of bread for me.

Knock, knock.
Who's there?
Cronkite.
Cronkite who?
Cronkite evidence.

Knock, knock.
Who's there?
Julia.
Julia who?
Julia want some milk and cookies?

Knock, knock.
Who's there?
General!
General who?

General Lee I don't mind school lunches!

Knock, knock.
Who's there?
Tad.
Tad who?
Tad old black magic.

Knock, knock.
Who's there?
Zinka!
Zinka who?
Zinka da ship!

Knock, knock.
Who's there?
Eamon.
Eamon who?
Eamon in a good mood today, come in...

Knock, knock.
Who's there?
Gerald.
Gerald who?
Gerald washed up!

Knock, knock.
Who's there?
Keith.
Keith who?
Keith your hands off of me!

Knock, knock.
Who's there?
Tariq.
Tariq who?
Tariq of perfume.

Knock, knock.
Who's there?
Mustache.
Mustache who?
Mustache–I'm in a hurry.

Knock, knock.
Who's there?
Candy.
Candy who?
Candy cow jump over the moon?

Knock, knock.
Who's there?
Dad.
Dad who?
Dad fuel to the fire!

Knock, knock.
Who's there?
Queen.
Queen who?
Queen as a whistle!

Knock, knock.
Who's there?
Duck.
Duck who?

Da cuckoo fell out of da clock!

Knock, knock.
Who's there?
Vampire!
Vampire who?
Vampire state building!

Knock, knock.
Who's there?
Bacon.
Bacon who?
Bacon a cake for your birthday.

Knock, knock.
Who's there?
Wade.
Wade who?
Wade till next time.

Knock, knock.
Who's there?
Leaf.
Leaf who?
Leaf me alone.

Knock, knock.
Who's there?
Yoga.
Yoga who?
Yoga what it takes!

Knock, knock.
Who's there?
Yolanda.
Yolanda who?
Yolanda me some money?

Knock, knock.
Who's there?
Hacienda!
Hacienda who?
Hacienda the story!

Knock, knock.
Who's there?
Howie!
Howie who!
I'm fine, how are you!

KNOCK, KNOCK.
WHO'S THERE?
JEFFERSON.
JEFFERSON WHO?

JEFFERSON YOURSELF ON A SUN DECK?

Knock, knock.
Who's there?
Myth.
Myth who?
Myth me while I'm gone?

Knock, knock.
Who's there?
Marcus!
Marcus who?
Marcus a book in the Bible!

Knock, knock.
Who's there?
Maida.
Maida who?
Maida force be with you!

Knock, knock.
Who's there?
Jacklyn.
Jacklyn who?
Jacklyn Hyde!

KNOCK, KNOCK.
WHO'S THERE?
HENNA.
HENNA WHO?

HENNA THING YOU WANT.

Knock, knock.
Who's there?
Sherwood!
Sherwood who!
Sherwood like to come in!

Knock, knock.
Who's there?
Shirley!
Shirley who?
Shirley you must know
me by now!

KNOCK, KNOCK.
WHO'S THERE?
SPIN.
SPIN WHO?
SPIN A LONG TIME SINCE WE LAST MET.

KNOCK, KNOCK.
WHO'S THERE?
STU.
STU WHO?
STU CLOSE FOR COMFORT.

Knock, knock.
Who's there?
Toby.

Toby who?
Toby or not to be–that is the question.

Knock, knock.
Who's there?
Duey.
Duey who?
Duey have to keep telling knock-knock jokes?

The end!